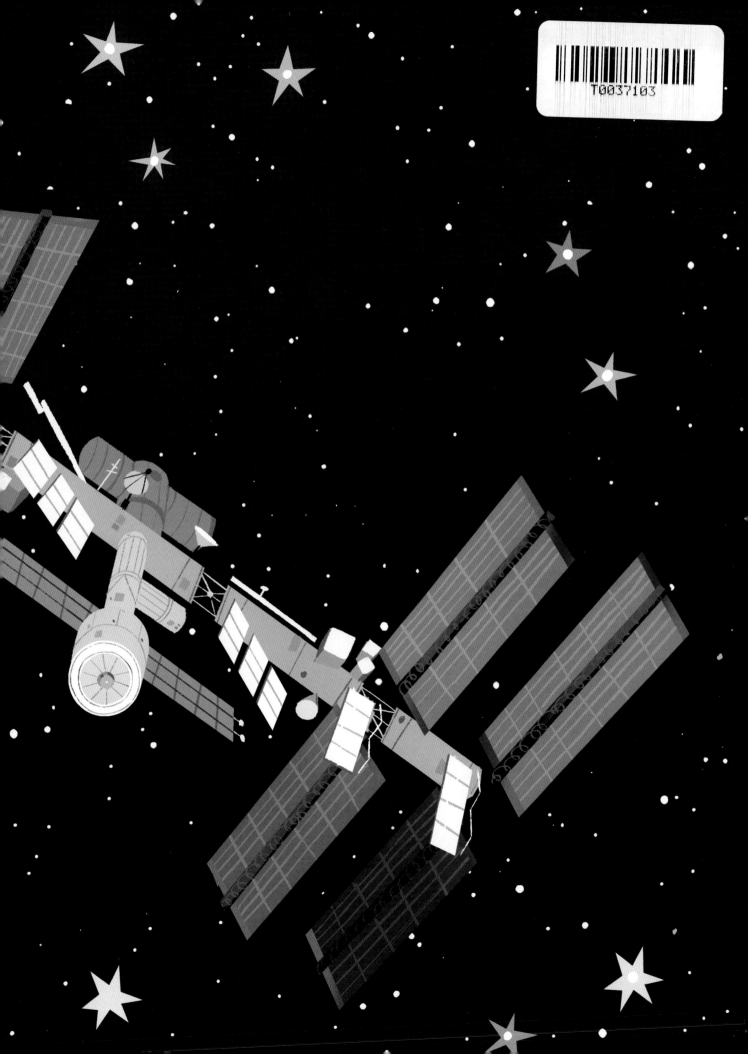

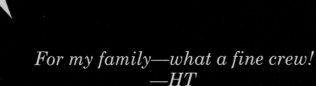

For my family—what a fine crew!
—HT

For all the young astronauts out there, dreaming to explore the stars.
—SL

Many thanks to Kimberly Glaus Läte of the Space Food Systems Laboratory at NASA Johnson Space Center and Dr. Gioia Massa, Plant Scientist at NASA Kennedy Space Center, for generously sharing their time and expertise.

About This Book

The illustrations for this book were rendered digitally. This book was edited by Samantha Gentry and designed by Brenda E. Angelilli. The production was supervised by Patricia Alvarado, and the production editor was Jake Regier. The text was set in Century Schoolbook, and the display type is Billy.

Text copyright © 2023 by Helen Taylor • Illustrations copyright © 2023 by Stevie Lewis • Cover illustration copyright © 2023 by Stevie Lewis • Cover design by Brenda E. Angelilli • Cover copyright © 2023 by Hachette Book Group, Inc. • Hachette Book Group supports the right to free expression and the value of copyright. The purpose of copyright is to encourage writers and artists to produce the creative works that enrich our culture. • The scanning, uploading, and distribution of this book without permission is a theft of the author's intellectual property. If you would like permission to use material from the book (other than for review purposes), please contact permissions@hbgusa.com. Thank you for your support of the author's rights. • Little, Brown and Company • Hachette Book Group • 1290 Avenue of the Americas, New York, NY 10104 • Visit us at LBYR.com • First Edition: October 2023 • Little, Brown and Company is a division of Hachette Book Group, Inc. • The Little, Brown name and logo are trademarks of Hachette Book Group, Inc. • The publisher is not responsible for websites (or their content) that are not owned by the publisher. • Photos on pages 34–35 copyright © by NASA • Little, Brown and Company books may be purchased in bulk for business, educational, or promotional use. For information, please contact your local bookseller or the Hachette Book Group Special Markets Department at special.markets@hbgusa.com. • Library of Congress Cataloging-in-Publication Data • Names: Taylor, Helen Springhetti, 1982– author. | Lewis, Stevie, illustrator. • Title: How to eat in space / by Helen Taylor ; illustrated by Stevie Lewis. • Description: First edition. | New York : Little, Brown and Company, 2023. | Includes bibliographical references. | Audience: Ages 4–8 | Summary: "A kid-friendly, accessible, and humorous text that describes the sometimes complicated task of eating while in space." —Provided by publisher. • Identifiers: LCCN 2021040942 | ISBN 9780316367745 (hardcover) • Subjects: LCSH: Space stations—Juvenile literature. | Menus for space flight—Juvenile literature. • Classification: LCC TL797.15 .T39 2023 | DDC 629.44/2—dc23 • LC record available at https://lccn.loc.gov/2021040942 • ISBN 978-0-316-36774-5 • PRINTED IN CHINA • APS • 10 9 8 7 6 5 4 3 2 1

How to Eat in Space

By Helen Taylor   Art by Stevie Lewis

LITTLE, BROWN AND COMPANY

New York   Boston

Welcome to the space station.
You're just in time for breakfast!
Heads up—you're speeding through
space at a whopping five miles per
second without a grocery store in
sight. Or a kitchen. Or even a plate.
Oh, and everything floats!

But don't worry.
With these tips and
tricks, you'll be dining
like an astronaut in
no time. Remain calm an

STICK TO THE MENU.

Feel like oatmeal? A smoothie? Scrambled eggs? Help yourself. You have hundreds of items to choose from. But watermelon? No way—too big, too heavy, too fresh!

Astronaut food must be
lightweight and packaged to last.
No refrigeration required.
So grab what you'd like from
the pantry and enjoy the view.

You're 250 miles above
Earth! Just remember . . .

EGGS

FOOD BELONGS IN YOUR MOUTH.

Sticky foods cling to forks and spoons, but loose bits like to wander. In the event of an egg escape or an oatmeal-glob gone rogue, perform a Midair Recapture Maneuver.

Gulp!

OATS

Thirsty? Nothing pours in space, so ordinary cups don't work. Instead, drinks come in pouches. Pick your favorite flavor; the powder's already inside. Just add water, a straw, and *voilà!*

💡**TIP** **To avoid a Leaky Lemonade Incident, clamp the straw shut between sips.**

Go ahead and play with your food. But don't go overboard—
secure those blobs and globs before . . .

Oh dear. You really must . . .

MIND YOUR MANNERS.

Apart from the occasional space walk outside, you'll spend a lot of time indoors with your crewmates. So avoid splats and don't eat all the cornflakes. Above all, be nice.

Speaking of common courtesy . . .

KEEP IT TIDY.

Tiny crumbs can float into eyes or instrument panels and cause huge problems. So crackers and cookies must stay bite-size. And instead of bread, you'll eat tortillas. A *lot* of tortillas.

TIP Get a grip. To keep your cashews from slipping away, clip the packet to the table. Or stick it to your pants! Every bottle, pouch, and jar—even the peanut butter lid—has a fuzzy fastener preattached.

FUZZY FASTENER

TERIYAKI

MAYO

KETCHUP

GREEN TEA

BERRY MEDLEY

SALMON

PEANUT BUTTER

S

BUNGEE CORD

ORANGE JUICE

...IED PORK

P

CARROTS

MAC & CHEESE

GREEN BEANS

CANDY

CLIPS

DRIED PEARS

TAPE, STICKY SIDE UP

BEEF PATTY

CASHEWS

While neatness is essential, don't let it hold you back. Be creative and . . .

MIX IT UP.
Try ketchup on your carrots.
Eat lunch upside down.
Or take time to treat
yourself! When food floats,
it's simplest to eat one thing
at a time. But with a dash
of extra effort, you could
assemble a space burrito. . . .

BEEF ENCHILADAS

Just secure your tortilla to the table. Then spread on the beans and cheese—s l o w l y (so they stick)—and add salsa. Go mild if you must, but you may prefer a spicy kick. Many astronauts report a weaker sense of taste while in orbit.

Now find a toehold (sorry, no sitting!) and dig in.

Or live large and . . .

Once in a while, your pals on Earth will send up a surprise—
apples, oranges, maybe an onion or two. Even better: pizza-
making ingredients! On such an occasion, be sure to invite the
whole crew. Good food tastes better with good company.

FROM:
EARTH

HANDLE
WITH CARE

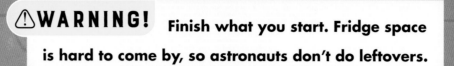

On that note, please . . .

BE WATER WISE.

Water is heavy and expensive to launch into space, so every droplet counts. Guzzle up all traces of hot cocoa. Save each driblet of sweat, every ounce of pee.

That's right. After some seriously high-tech filtration, you'll drink it again. Wash your hair with it. And brush your teeth with it. But don't be a water hog. . . .

BEEF JERKY

SNACK CAKES

CHOCOLATE

MIXED NUTS

SEAWEED

MARSHMALLOW
CREME

MISO RAMEN

DRIED
PICKLES

TAHINI

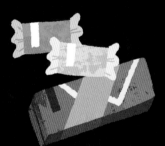

CANDY

SHARING IS CARING.

The pantry is stocked with food and drinks for everyone. Astronauts also get "bonus boxes" packed with their personal favorites. *Mmmmmm.* What's in yours?

Taste buds feeling tired? Swap snacks with a
crewmate from another country to liven things up.
At dinnertime, do yourself a favor and . . .

PRACTICE PATIENCE.
You won't need to cook, but prepping dinner still takes time.

Feel like asparagus? Inject fifty milliliters of hot water into the pouch and massage it gently. Rehydration takes ten minutes.

Hungry for lasagna? Switch on the food warmer. In twenty minutes, *beep beep*—time to eat! Snip an X to open the package the flaps help your food stay put between bites.

TIP Tackle those to-reach corners wi extra-long spoon!

GROW YOUR OWN SALAD.

Ahhh, the satisfying crunch of fresh lettuce. Up here, loose soil could cause chaos, so your seedlings will emerge from pillows of clay and fertilizer.

PLANT PILLOW

They'll grow toward electric lights because windows are scarce. Plus, the Sun rises and sets sixteen times *a day*—once for each lap around Earth.

At harvest time, save a sample to study—you *are* conducting a scientific experiment, after all. Then clean the remaining leaves (who knows what *else* might be growing on there) and enjoy!

Hopefully you remembered to . . .

SAVE ROOM FOR DESSERT.

Gobble up some cobbler, bite into a brownie, or whip up a space s'more. You could even score the gourmet creation of a famous chef!

All done? Don't just float there. . . .

CLEAN UP AFTER YOURSELF.

Bad news: There's no sink.

Good news: There are no dishes to wash, either!

Just wipe down your silverware and sort your trash.

Bundle wet waste tightly in its own bag to keep the station from getting stinky.

⚠️**WARNING!** Do. Not. Skip. This. Step. Trash day may be weeks or even months away, and these windows don't open!

TRASH #39

As you circle Earth once more before bedtime . . .

THANK YOUR LUCKY STARS.

Early space explorers ate gel-coated sandwich cubes and sloppy-joe smoothies from a tube. Yuck! So you are one fortunate astronaut.

Plus, before long you'll head home, sit down in a *real* chair at a *real* table, and eat the freshest, messiest meal imaginable. On a plate! In the meantime, sweet dreams and bon appétit.

HUNGRY FOR MORE?

The strategies in this book for eating while away from Earth come from real life—specifically, from the people who live and work on the International Space Station (ISS), and from the food scientists and nutritionists who support them. The station, whose first modules launched in 1998, grew out of a partnership between the United States, Russia, Europe, Japan, and Canada. Since the first crew arrived in 2000, more than 250 people from twenty countries (and counting) have visited it. While living onboard, crew members conduct scientific experiments, care for the station and themselves, and of course work up an appetite!

Now that you know *how* astronauts eat in space, let's dig into *why* they do it that way. . . .

SAFETY FIRST.

On Earth, we cook with stoves and ovens and store perishable food in fridges and freezers. In space, such luxuries aren't available. So astronaut food is carefully prepared on Earth, then flown up in batches. Some items are freeze-dried; others are sealed up, then sterilized with heat or a zap of radiation. These preservation methods make food safe to store at room temperature and eat right out of the package. Some space agencies use flexible pouches, while others use cans; both kinds of packaging block light, air, and moisture so bacteria can't grow.

When an entire menu is prepackaged, balancing nutritional needs gets complicated. For instance, vitamin C, which prevents scurvy (among other things), can't handle heat. Fortunately, it's stable when dehydrated, so astronauts get plenty of vitamin C in powdered drinks, which of course require . . .

WATER, PRECIOUS WATER.

To reduce the number of fresh gallons needed from Earth, all water on the ISS is recycled again and again. NASA, the United States' space agency, designed a system to collect each drop of exhaled moisture, sweat, and pee, and clean it for reuse. Their goal: 98 percent efficiency, the level required for longer-duration missions someday. As astronauts like to joke, today's coffee is tomorrow's coffee. (Or orange juice!) Unusual as it sounds, the station's filtered water is cleaner than most tap water on Earth.

The water spigot in the galley (that's station-speak for *kitchen*) has two settings: hot and room temperature. However, with a little planning, astronauts can enjoy an occasional sip of cold H_2O. The station's limited refrigerated space is primarily for sensitive research materials. But astronauts get to share two shoebox-size chillers for drinks, perishable condiments, and snacks that taste best cool, such as shrimp cocktail. It's a nice perk, since . . .

FROM: EARTH

HANDLE WITH CARE

NOTHING BEATS FRESH PRODUCE.

Spacecraft transport supplies, experiments, and equipment to the space station. Sometimes they also deliver small quantities of fresh fruits and vegetables. Apples and carrots are popular because they're crunchy *and* durable. Oh, and nutritious too!

Future long-distance missions, however, won't include grocery deliveries. So astronauts are learning to grow their own produce in two chambers: Veggie and its larger, more automated cousin, the Advanced Plant Habitat. Initial harvests have included cabbage, bok choy, lettuce, and kale.

Flowering plants, such as peppers, tomatoes, and strawberries, present some unique challenges. They're thirstier than leafy greens, and they require pollination to bear fruit. Without Earth's gravity (or space bees) to assist, astronauts may need to hand-paint pollen from one flower to another! Research is ongoing, but early results indicate that ISS-grown peppers taste great on tacos.

Space-grown produce won't replace prepackaged foods anytime soon, but it's a valuable addition, in part because . . .

TASTE MATTERS.

Meals in space need to be more than nutritious and edible—they must be appealing! The healthiest, best-balanced meal in the universe is useless if astronauts won't eat it.

Food scientists design recipes and packaging to maintain nutrition, texture, and flavor for as long as possible. Still, quality degrades over time. That's why food scientists test extensively for safety and enjoyability. Rehydratable kale salad? A welcome addition to the menu. Thermostabilized cheesecake? Didn't make the cut—the texture just wasn't quite right.

For the astronauts' health, recipes are light on salt, sugar, and fat. These limitations make battling bland flavors extra tricky. Plus, one effect of weightlessness is that astronauts tend to have stuffy noses, which can dull the taste of food. Hot sauce helps. But for crunch . . .

VARIETY IS KEY.

A typical mission to the ISS lasts six months. Some last up to a year. Eating the same thing day after day would get old fast. And astronauts struggling with "menu fatigue" might not eat enough.

In the past, astronauts customized their meal plans in advance, but the system proved too complicated. Now the station's pantry is stocked with a wide variety of choices to keep things interesting—from rhubarb applesauce to curried pumpkin soup. Not all space agencies have a dedicated food production system, but *every* astronaut has the opportunity to fly with foods that reflect their culture's cuisine. For instance, before South Korea's first astronaut headed to the ISS, its food scientists developed a space-friendly recipe for kimchi, a spicy fermented cabbage dish traditionally served at most meals.

Astronauts' "bonus boxes" contain even more personalized goodies. Favorite snacks, beloved treats from childhood, hometown specialties—as long as they meet safety requirements, they're fair game. Far away from family and friends, those familiar flavors can be comforting. Plus . . .

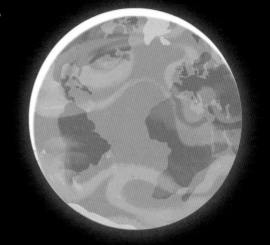

TREATS ROCK!

Sometimes astronauts partner with famous chefs, creating unique meals to share on special occasions. For example, French astronaut Thomas Pesquet once brought food prepared by Michelin-star chef Alain Ducasse, including lobster, potato cakes with wild mushrooms, and almond tarts with caramelized pears. Gourmet menus aside, many astronauts simply value the camaraderie of eating meals together. It's more like home.

One treat astronauts don't eat: the freeze-dried "astronaut ice cream" found in museum gift shops. But occasionally, they do get real ice cream! When an experiment needs to stay frozen on its way back to Earth, NASA flies a small freezer up to the station. Instead of sending it empty, they'll stash a sweet surprise inside because . . .

THERE'S NO TASTE LIKE HOME.

On longer journeys, reminders of life on Earth will become even more important. Someday astronauts might even enjoy fresh-baked cookies! In an initial experiment, five chocolate chip cookies, each tucked into a silicone pouch, were baked inside a cylindrical oven for 25 to 130 minutes. The results were frozen and shipped to Earth for analysis—no taste-testing allowed until all the kinks are worked out.

Ovens and freezers could be transformative for astronaut cuisine. But they also use power and take up room—both of which are in short supply on spacecraft. Further analysis will reveal which trade-offs are worth making. Whatever the fate of space cookies, one thing is certain. . . .

THE FUTURE BECKONS.

The ISS orbits about 250 miles above Earth's surface, where fresh supplies are a short rocket ride away. But NASA and other space agencies are working to send astronauts back to the Moon's surface (250 *thousand* miles away) and to Mars (35 to 250 *million* miles away). Spacecraft that far out must be self-sufficient.

A round-trip mission to Mars will likely last two to three years. It will require new strategies in many areas, including food science. NASA's goals include producing more fresh food in space with minimal water and power use, and extending the shelf life of prepackaged foods to at least five years. The most promising concepts will be tested on the ISS, future space stations, and the Moon.

Growing a space pepper or fine-tuning a tricky recipe might seem like small potatoes, but it's all part of a grander plan. To tackle the "big" questions, like *What's out there?*, we must start with simpler ones: *What's for dinner?*

KEEP EXPLORING

In Books

Floca, Brian. *Moonshot: The Flight of Apollo 11.* Atheneum Books for Young Readers, 2009.

Gregory, Josh. *If You Were a Kid Docking at the International Space Station.* Scholastic Inc., 2017.

Kelly, Scott. *My Journey to the Stars.* Crown Books for Young Readers, 2017.

Lapin, Joyce. *If You Had Your Birthday Party on the Moon.* Sterling Children's Books, 2019.

Read, John A. *50 Things to Know About the International Space Station.* Formac, 2021.

Online

Tour the International Space Station: https://www.youtube.com/watch?v=tBVUTFPate0

Find activities and games in NASA Kids' Club: https://nasa.gov/kidsclub

See astronauts share their daily routines: https://nasa.gov/audience/foreducators/stem-on-station/dayinthelife

Watch an astronaut make a peanut butter and jelly sandwich in space: https://www.youtube.com/watch?v=Z2szk-NuKWg

In Person

Spot the International Space Station passing over your hometown: https://spotthestation.nasa.gov

K–12 classrooms in the United States and Canada can grow tomatoes from seeds that have visited space as part of an
ongoing research project: http://tomatosphere.org

SELECTED SOURCES

Bourland, Charles T., and Gregory L. Vogt. *The Astronaut's Cookbook: Tales, Recipes, and More.* Springer New York, 2010.

Carter, Noelle. "Col. Chris Hadfield: An astronaut's guide to eating in space." *The Splendid Table,* January 24, 2014.
https://splendidtable.org/story/2014/01/24/col-chris-hadfield-an-astronauts-guide-to-eating-in-space.

Chang, Kenneth. "It's Dinner Time on the Space Station. Lobster or Beef Bourguignon?" *The New York Times,* April 22, 2021.
Updated August 2, 2021. https://www.nytimes.com/2021/04/22/science/astronauts-food-space-station.html.

Cranford, Nathan A., and Jennifer L. Turner. "The Menu for Mars: Designing a Deep Space Food System." NASA, March 25, 2021.
https://nasa.gov/feature/the-menu-for-mars-designing-a-deep-space-food-system.

"Dining on the Space Station." NASA Johnson. YouTube, December 30, 2010. https://youtube.com/watch?v=PLmc6CJQwLM.

"ISS Update: Packing and Preparing Space Food (Part 2)." NASA Johnson. YouTube, November 21, 2012.
https://youtube.com/watch?v=rbnipg_DsJk.

Jordan, Gary. "Episode 4: Space Food." *Houston We Have a Podcast.* NASA, July 28, 2017.
https://www.nasa.gov/johnson/HWHAP/space-food.

Koren, Marina. "Everything You Never Thought to Ask About Astronaut Food." *The Atlantic,* December 15, 2017.
https://www.theatlantic.com/science/archive/2017/12/astronaut-food-international-space-station/548255/.

Lupo, Lisa. "Food in Space: Defying (Micro)Gravity to Feed Our Astronauts." *Quality Assurance Magazine,* May 21, 2018.
http://qualityassurancemag.com/article/food-space-defying-microgravity-feed-astronauts/.

Magnus, Sandra. "Food and Cooking in Space." ISS Expedition 18. NASA, updated October 23, 2010.
https://nasa.gov/mission_pages/station/expeditions/expedition18/journal_sandra_magnus_6.html.

Uri, John. "Space Station 20th: Food on ISS." NASA, August 14, 2020. https://nasa.gov/feature/space-station-20th-food-on-iss.

"Veggie." NASA, accessed August 11, 2021. https://nasa.gov/sites/default/files/atoms/files/veggie_fact_sheet_508.pdf.

▶ Surrounded by food and drink packets, NASA astronaut Leland Melvin heads home on the now-retired space shuttle Atlantis.

▲ Aboard the ISS, NASA astronaut Kevin Ford's image is refracted in a floating water bubble.

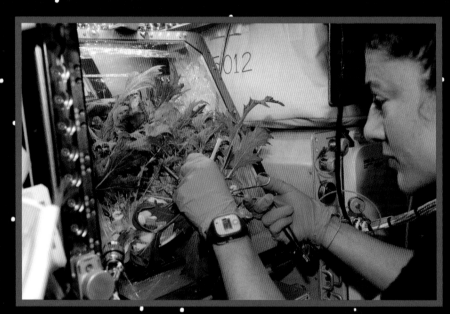

▲ NASA astronaut Jessica Meir harvests Mizuna mustard greens grown under LED lights in the Veggie chamber.

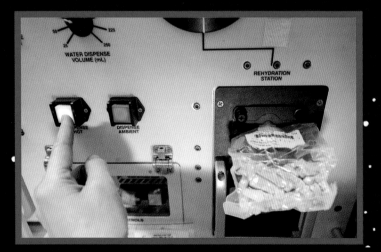

▲ Freeze-dried green beans with mushrooms are rehydrated with hot water.

▲ Before leaving Earth, crew members at NASA's Johnson Space Center try to rate everything on the menu in the food lab.